KU-256-598

Contents

Copyright © MCMLXXXVII by Cliveden Press.
All rights reserved throughout the world.
Published by Cliveden Press,
An Egmont Company, Egmont House, P.O. Box 111,
Great Ducie Street, Manchester M60 3BL.
Printed in Hungary. SBN 7235 7296 8.

DINOSAUR WORLD

Written by Glynis Langley.

Illustrated by Mike Atkinson.

CLIVEDEN PRESS

THE WORLD OF THE DINOSAURS

To imagine the world of the dinosaurs, first cast your mind back 200 million years . . .

Impossible, isn't it!

But it really was such an astonishingly long time ago when the first dinosaurs roamed the earth — an earth which these mighty creatures were to dominate for 140 million years.

Think of a dinosaur and you generally imagine one of the colossal, lumbering plant eaters, for instance the placid *Diplodocus,* or else a fierce and frightening flesh eater, such as the monstrous *Tyrannosaurus Rex,* the movie makers' favourite.

But they came in all shapes and sizes, with lifestyles and temperaments to match. You'll meet just a sample selection of the most interesting in the pages of this book — but there are many more which we know of, and no doubt others still of which as yet we have found no fossil evidence.

The three periods during which the dinosaurs lived — the Triassic, the Jurassic and the Cretaceous — were times of great change. There were changes in climate, and even changes in the earth's landmasses. Plant and animal life changed too.

But still the dinosaurs marched on. These fascinating creatures continued their reptilian reign until around 64 million years ago, when in a relatively short time they simply became extinct. No one quite knows why.

But that's another story.

For now, read on . . . and enter the long vanished world of those most intriguing of creatures — the dinosaurs.

AQUATIC ORIGINS

At the very dawn of history,
life began in the sea.

JELLYFISH

The familiar *jellyfish*
was one of the first animals
to have a stomach and a mouth.

MICRO-ORGANISMS

Thousands of millions of years ago,
protozoans were the first 'animals'.

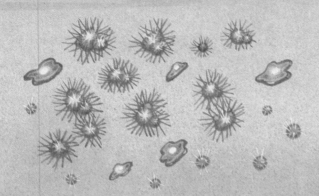

TRILOBITES

Invertebrates, feeding on
micro-organisms in the sand,
trilobites left clear
fossil remains.

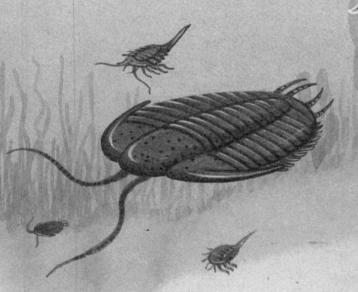

SPONGES

STARFISH

Further developed still,
starfish had a rudimentary
nervous system and brain.

WORMS

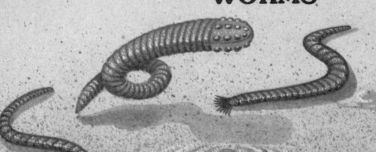

AMMONITES

The coiled shells of the *ammonites* are well known to fossil collectors.

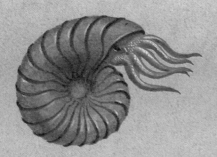

PLACODERMS

Next came the vertebrates, and the first true fish, the *placoderms*.

BELEMNITES

Relatives of the present-day cuttlefish, *belemnites* had distinctive patterns of stripes and zigzags on their shells.

DINICHTHYS

With a head measuring up to a metre long, this fearsome-looking fish was a successful predator.

NOTE:

Some of these creatures lived in freshwater as well as the sea, and not all would necessarily have been alive at the same time.

9

THE AMPHIBIANS

Three hundred and fifty million years ago, evolution took a big step forward.

Primitive fish of the *crossopterygian* group emerged from the water and started to move across the sand and mud, using their fins to push them along. This tremendously important development would 'soon' – that is, over a few million years! – lead to the group of animals we call amphibians.

They were able to live on land, but had to return to the water to lay their eggs, just like the familiar frogs and toads of today.

Eryops was a fairly typical swamp-dwelling amphibian.

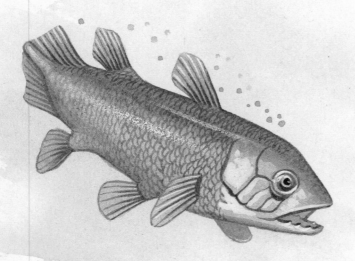

The *Coelacanth* is a member of the *crossopterygian* group. This is the fish which shook the scientific world in 1938, when it was rediscovered off Africa, after supposedly being extinct for 70 million years!

THE REPTILES

The next major development was the evolution of reptiles, who laid their eggs on land, and it is here that the dinosaur story really begins.

The first reptile, and the first ancestor of all the dinosaurs, was *Seymouria*, which looked like a small crocodile. Its own unremarkable appearance gave no clue to the weird and wonderful forms which were to follow!

GIANTS' GALLERY

ELASMOSAURUS

Seventy-six vertebra, or backbone segments. This is the largest number of any animal ever known.

Long neck could reach 7 m above surface of water, enabling *Elasmosaurus* to catch passing *pteranodons,* to supplement its diet of fish.

Fine, sharp teeth.

Comparatively small head.

Four paddle-like limbs for swimming agility, typical of the *plesiosaurs.*

Fossil remains show stones in stomach, possibly swallowed to help in some way with digestion of large fish.

Short tail.

FACTS AND FIGURES

Size: 12 m long
Gait: Fast and agile swimmer
Diet: Mainly fish
Meaning of name: Swan lizard

BACK TO THE WATER

After the emergence of those first primitive fish, and the development of reptiles on land, many millions of years went by before large reptiles began once more to adapt to the water as their environment.

A typical *pliosaur*

Two main groups of marine reptiles developed: the *ichthyosaurs* and the *plesiosaurs*.

The various types of animals in the two distinct groups were similar in many ways. All were very much at home in the water, though the *pliosaurs* – a division of the *plesiosaur* family – with their heavy bodies and short necks, were built more for long distance endurance than for aquatic agility.

Ichthyosaurus

Fish was the main diet for most of these marine reptiles, though some also dived in deeper water for *cephalopods*, a group of small creatures related to the squids of today. The *pliosaurs'* blunt teeth were particularly well adapted for this type of food, whereas the long necks of the *plesiosaurs* enabled them to turn quickly and snap at passing fish.

It is just one of the intriguing mysteries about early creatures that although all the scientific evidence points to the *ichthyosaurs* being all in all the best adapted to marine life, it was in fact the other group which became more successful.

Elasmosaurus, on page 11, was a *plesiosaur.*

BEFORE THE DINOSAURS . . .

Before the great age of the dinosaurs, mammals and reptiles began to develop along different lines. For a time – a few million years, that is! – reptilian creatures with some mammal-like features were dominant. They are sometimes called *parsamammals*.

DIMETRODON

Looking a lot like the storybook dragons of medieval times, *Dimetrodon's* terrifying appearance certainly reflected its fearsome and ferocious nature.

   Dimetrodon's dorsal fin was used to retain the sun's rays, which helped the animal to regulate its body temperature. Despite a popular myth, it did not propel *Dimetrodon* along like a sail!

Though small by dinosaur standards – about 3 metres long – *Dimetrodon* was exceptionally strong and ferocious. It would attack creatures almost as big as itself.

The modern-day sailfish also has an enormous dorsal fin.

If food was scarce, *Cynognathus* might have had to make do with insects. This would not have been such a hardship, as many of the insects of the time were quite large, and this small group of beetle-like insects would make a reasonable meal.

CYNOGNATHUS

The peculiar-looking *Cynognathus* was a real mixture between mammal and reptile. It had a hairy body – very much a mammalian characteristic – and yet it laid eggs, which of course is reptilian.

Its name means 'jaws of a dog', and it certainly did have a dog-like appearance, with its sharp teeth and four-footed stance, body held well off the ground. Like a dog too, it was no doubt fast and agile, and would have been a successful hunter.

MOSCHOPS

Despite its appearance, *Moschops* was actually a placid plant-eater, often browsing along the banks of rivers.

THE FIRST MAMMALS

Not much is known about the very first mammals, which lived alongside the dinosaurs.

They were probably small, shrew-like creatures, fast moving and agile, and may well have fed on dinosaur eggs.

They were the forerunners of a group of animals which were to develop into an astonishing variety of forms, including all the mammals we see around us today.

DISCOVERIES AND DISCOVERERS

Our vivid picture of the world of the dinosaurs has been built up like a gigantic jigsaw puzzle over several centuries.
Here are just some of the pieces.

THE CLERICAL CONNECTION!

For some reason, many important dinosaur finds in Britain have been made by clergymen, and indeed it was the Rev. Dr. Robert Plot, in 1676, who made the first ever recorded dinosaur discovery.

He came across part of a gigantic thigh bone in a quarry in Cornwall, but of course could not imagine the kind of animal whose bone it might have been. He assumed that it must be evidence of a race of giant men, and made several drawings of the bone, along with detailed descriptions.

It was lucky that he did, for over the years all trace of the bone has been lost. Experts who have studied the drawings, however, are fairly sure that the bone must have belonged to the great meat-eater, *Megalosaurus*.

It was in 1841 that Richard Owen — a brilliant anatomist who had done much work on the fossil finds — first coined the name *Dinosauria*. He described the creatures as "a distinct tribe or suborder of Saurian Reptiles", and chose the name because of its translation: 'terrible lizards'.

MARY ANNING AND THE MANTELLS

In early nineteenth century Britain, two names were prominent in the field of fossil hunting: Mary Anning and the Mantells.

Mary Anning began hunting for fossils as a girl of twelve, and made many important discoveries. She found a *pterosaur,* several *ichthyosaurs* and a *plesiosaur,* hidden in the fossil-rich rocks of Lyme Regis in Dorset.

Dr. Gideon Mantell and his wife Mary were also keen fossil-hunters, but their most important find was quite by chance. Dr. Mantell was visiting a patient in Lewes, Sussex, and whilst he was busy Mary Mantell went for a walk.

Lying in a pile of rubble by the side of the road were a number of large fossil teeth. They were quite unlike anything in the Mantells' collections, and Dr. Mantell embarked on research about them which was to take him several years.

Tracing the teeth to a quarry, they found further parts of the animal, and as time went by became more and more convinced that the finds were proof of the existence of huge, plant-eating reptiles. Few people believed them!

Dr. Mantell called this reptile *Iguanodon,* because the teeth resembled those of the iguana lizard, though the two animals are not related.

THE BERNISSART BONES

Probably the most spectacular find in Europe came in 1877, when coal miners at Bernissart in Belgium started to find huge skeletons in their excavations.

The bones were investigated by a scientist named Louis Dollo, though at the outset no one could have imagined what an exciting find it would prove to be. In all, 31 complete skeletons were found, all of *Iguanodon,* the creature identified by Dr. Mantell. Apparently this was the evidence of a great disaster which had befallen a whole tribe of *Iguanodon* — possibly they had fallen down a ravine — and it was a tremendously important find.

Dr. Mantell had been working from a pile of assorted bones in his attempts to reconstruct the appearance of *Iguanodon.* Puzzled by a small bony spike, he eventually decided that this must have been a horn on the creature's snout. The complete skeletons from Bernissart revealed the truth — it was *Iguanodon's* distinctive thumb bone.

FOSSIL HUNTING U.S. STYLE!

The pioneering spirit was everywhere in the USA in the late nineteenth century — not least in the world of fossil hunting. Teams of collectors struck out cross country in covered wagons, ready for days and nights on the dinosaur trail. Leaders in the field were Othniel Charles Marsh and Edward Drinker Cope.

Marsh and Cope were both brilliant scientists and palaeontologists, both working along the same general lines of research. But the men were totally different in character, and before long a bitter feud had developed between them, leading to what has been called the Cope-Marsh War.

Both men regularly set out with teams of fossil collectors, and the rivalry to make the best finds was intense, leading to spying, bribery and all manner of other ruses between the teams.

Despite the 'war' however, both men made many important finds, and contributed vastly to scientific understanding of dinosaurs. The amount of material they studied was vast: one excavation site yielded a tonne of fossils every week for nearly ten years!

Those dramatic fossil hunting days left their mark on America. In Colorado today there is a town called Dinosaur, which boasts a Brontosaurus Boulevard!

DINOSAUR FINDS IN THE GOBI DESERT

The Gobi Desert in Mongolia has proved to be a marvellous location for dinosaur fossil hunting, and several important expeditions have travelled there.

The first one, an American expedition in 1922, made many exciting discoveries, but perhaps the most notable was of some dinosaur eggs. This proved beyond all doubt what scientists had long believed to be the truth – that dinosaurs were egg-laying.

Other expeditions over the years made fascinating finds – such as a skeleton of the very rare *Psittacosaurus* – but it was a find in 1971 which was really to catch the imagination of the scientific world and the public alike.

Skeletons of the plant eater *Protoceratops* and the flesh eater *Velociraptor* were found – locked in deadly combat! These specimens remain to this day the only real evidence of dinosaurs fighting, and to find them preserved in the very act of battle was a spectacular discovery indeed.

Our artist's reconstruction of the dramatic find at Tugreeg in the Gobi Desert shows a fight which took place some 70 million years ago!

. . . AND STILL TODAY

From the fantastic amount of research which has been done, you might be tempted to imagine that scientists know all there is to know about the world of dinosaurs.

Far from it!

There is still a tremendous amount to be learned before we can add the final pieces to our jigsaw puzzle. Important finds are being made every year, and there is no doubt that many more intriguing facts will emerge as newly-discovered material is studied.

Who knows what intriguing secrets the fossil rocks still hold?

THE PLANT EATERS

The plant eaters were the biggest group of dinosaurs — in more ways than one!

Over the next few pages we take a look at some of them. But first, there's a big question mark hanging over the most colossal creatures . . .

WERE THEY SWAMP DWELLERS?

Until quite recently it was widely believed that the huge plant eating dinosaurs, such as *Diplodocus* and *Brachiosaurus,* lived mainly in swamps and rivers, using the water to support more comfortably their great weight. This is how they are often pictured in books, but nowadays the idea is seriously in doubt.

Their legs, after all, were of exactly the right strength and structure to support their weight, so why should the water be necessary? And then there is the shape of their feet: an animal spending its time wading about in the soft mud of a swamp would surely have to have wide, spreading feet to prevent it constantly sinking in — but the feet of the huge plant eaters were usually compact, with short, stubby toes.

The fact that the plant eaters had their nostrils on the top of their heads gives weight to the swamp dwelling theory, because it would mean that they could still breathe whilst under water. But of course there is a very successful land animal alive today which has similar nasal openings, and which does not live in water. It's the elephant, and interestingly, some of the plant eating *sauropods* may have had a proboscis similar to the elephant's trunk.

Some experts believe that these giant creatures lived around the edges of swamps, rivers and lakes, and may indeed have taken to the water at times to escape from predatory flesh eaters, but actually spent more of their time on land than wading in the depths.

Was *Camarasaurus* a wader?

SAUROPODS AND ORNITHOPODS

Melanosaurus was a typical *sauropod*. It walked on all fours, had heavy bones, a long neck, and a small head.

Ornithopods usually walked on their two back legs, though some could bend down and walk on all fours. *Camptosaurus* is a good example.

Plant life all those millions of years ago wasn't that much different from today. There were ferns, mosses and conifers in abundance, though grass and flowers did not appear till later. The plant-eating dinosaurs probably ate various kinds of vegetation, and they often browsed on the tough leaves of palm-like trees called *cycads*.

DIPLODOCUS 26.5 metres long
APATOSAURUS 21 metres long

(popularly known as *Brontosaurus*)

These two gentle giants had small heads – housing remarkably small brains! Despite their great size, they were no match for their great enemies, the fierce flesh eaters.

FOOTNOTE!

A preserved *Apatosaurus* footprint can hold 80 litres of water!

BRACHIOSAURUS

Nostrils: high up on the skull.

Brachiosaurus had an incredibly small brain.

Long, flexible neck: to reach vegetation growing at different levels.

Heavy body: accounting for much of its immense weight.

Front legs longer than the hind legs.

Small feet: (relatively speaking!)

Tail: useful for balance, and also possibly to lash out at enemy flesh eaters.

Small, peg-like teeth for grinding vegetation.

FACTS AND FIGURES

Size: 12 m tall, 30 m long
Weight: 80 tonnes
Gait: Clumsy and very slow (2 m.p.h.)
Diet: Vegetation – and plenty of it!
Meaning of name: Arm lizard (because of its huge front legs, or 'arms')

THE DUCK-BILLS

These were a very strange-looking group of dinosaurs!

The biggest of them all, *Anatosaurus*, is shown here. Its name means 'duck lizard', and, as you can see, its wide, flattened jaws do give the appearance of a duck's beak!

Anatosaurus had webbed front feet, and was probably a good swimmer.

Some of its relatives were stranger-looking still . . .

The bone-headed PACHYCEPHALOSAURUS had an extraordinary dome-shaped skull made of solid bone. With its lumpy, bumpy face it was not exactly the most handsome of dinosaurs. Its name translates as 'thick-headed lizard'!

LAMBEOSAURUS and CORYTHOSAURUS

had distinctive crests, the exact purpose of which is not known.

WEIRD AND WONDERFUL!

The *stegosaurs* and the *anklyosaurs* evolved a very effective way of protecting themselves from attack by flesh eaters . . . they wore coats of 'armour'!

KENTROSAURUS

was a *stegosaur*. It had spikes running down its back, and several on its tail.

CHIALINGOSAURUS

was a *stegosaur*. It had two rows of heavy bone plates on its back, and four sharp spikes on its tail.

NODOSAURUS

was an *anklyosaur*. Its name means 'knobbed lizard', and refers to the round lumps of hard bone all over its back.

The *ceratopsians,* or horned and frilled dinosaurs, were another bizarre-looking bunch!

The bony frill probably had a dual purpose. It would be alarming for another creature to look at, and therefore would give protection, but it would also increase the strength of the jaw muscles, allowing the *ceratopsians* to eat tougher plant foods.

They were mostly about the size of an elephant.

TRICERATOPS

The biggest of all the *ceratopsians, Triceratops* weighed 8 tonnes. This formidable animal was a match for even the fiercest flesh eaters, who would probably have simply turned tail and run from a charging *Triceratops!*

MONOCLONIUS

GIANTS' GALLERY

IGUANODON

Several rows of teeth along each jaw: new ones grew immediately to replace those lost.

Long tongue to reach out for vegetation.

Well developed hands: could possibly hold food.

Large webbed feet made it easier for *Iguanodon* to walk on soft ground.

Sharp spiky 'thumb' on each hand: this unusual feature was probably used for defence. If *Iguanodon* was unable to outrun a predator it could defend itself with stabbing blows from the spike.

Very large, muscular tail.

FACTS AND FIGURES

Size: 5m tall, 10m long
Weight: 5 tonnes
Gait: Quite agile. Iguanodon travelled in herds.
Diet: Vegetation
Meaning of name: Iguana tooth (though it is actually no relation to the iguana)

THE UNANSWERED QUESTIONS

Considering how long ago dinosaurs lived, it is remarkable that scientists have been able to discover so much about these fascinating animals, and their way of life. Inevitably though, some questions remain unanswered . . .

HOW BIG WERE DINOSAUR FAMILIES?

Though fossil finds have yielded evidence about the family life of some specific dinosaurs, we don't by any means have a clear general understanding of how they organised their family groups.

Did the young stay with or near their parents once they were able to fend for themselves? Were old dinosaurs 'looked after' by younger members of the family? Were many species solitary, coming together only to breed? And who looked after the young – male or female dinosaur?

What we do know for sure from fossil footprints is that some species – notably the large *sauropods* – moved about in herds, sometimes travelling great distances, presumably in the search for better feeding grounds. *Plateosaurus,* shown here, is thought to have been the first of the dinosaurs to herd.

DID DINOSAURS HIBERNATE?

The short answer is: we don't know! Some species may have done, or indeed they may have slept during the summer months instead, to escape oppressively hot weather.

COULD THERE HAVE BEEN A BIGGER DINOSAUR STILL?

Meet Supersaurus!

That's the apt nickname which has been coined for a creature which was probably even bigger than *Brachiosaurus,* for many years thought to have been the largest land animal ever.

Fossil remains of this colossal creature were first discovered in the Dry Mesa Quarry in western Colorado, USA, in 1971. Much work has still to be done, but it seems likely that the animal was a relative of *Brachiosaurus* – on an even more gigantic scale!

If the animal is proved to have been of the same general structure as its relative, you can see here how big it would be in comparision with a man. It probably weighed in at a useful 100 tonnes!

WARM-BLOODED OR COLD?

Debate about this one rages ever more hotly in scientific circles, and each theory has its own enthusiastic supporters!

The arguments are much too complex to go into here – it would take all the pages of this book to mention them all! – but if you're as intrigued by this as the experts are you'll find plenty of technical dinosaur books in your library which devote whole chapters to the subject.

Beware though . . . you'll probably read the first one and think 'yes, that sounds convincing'. But wait till you read the second, then the third . . .

THE FLESH EATERS

When most people think of dinosaurs they think of the savage, vicious creatures usually portrayed in exciting cinema films. And, of course, the flesh eaters *were* like that. But surprisingly, they were in the minority, with the placid plant eaters making up by far the bigger group.

The earliest flesh eaters were quite small – but nonetheless ferocious – creatures, hunting their prey with great speed and agility. As the millions of years passed by, larger and larger forms developed, culminating in impressive animals such as *Tyrannosaurus Rex,* towards the end of the age of the dinosaurs.

All the flesh eaters walked on their hind legs, using their short forelegs to hold and tear at their prey. Their tails were important for balance.

Obviously the larger creatures would not have been as nimble as the smaller ones, but what they lacked in speed they more than made up for in their awesome size and strength.

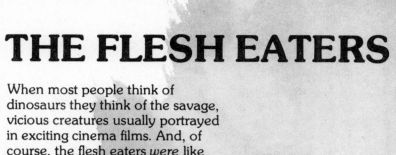

COELOPHYSIS

This animal was one of the first of all the dinosaurs. Experts know a great deal about it, because a large number of skeletons have been found.

Interestingly, some of these finds showed evidence that the animals had fed on others of their own kind, indicating that the savagery of *Coelophysis* did not stop short of cannibalism.

SMALL – BUT DEADLY!

ORNITHOMIMUS

Ornithomimus is interesting for several reaons, one – or rather two! – of which were its long, spindly forearms. They were almost like a human being's arms.

Something which would seem to be a great disadvantage for a flesh eating dinosaur was the fact that *Ornithomimus* had no teeth! It probably fed on worms and small lizards, which it swallowed whole, and also broke into eggs with its powerful beak.

It may also have eaten some plant material, for instance fruit.

COMPSOGNATHUS

The smallest of all known dinosaurs. Compsognathus would have eaten small prey like insects and lizards, and also possibly food such as dead fish washed up on the shore.

For a small creature, it has an impressive name, meaning 'boastful jaw'.

A recently discovered *Compsognathus* skeleton – found in West Germany – poses some intriguing questions. It contains what appears to be the skeleton of another, much smaller *Compsognathus*, right in the middle of the larger animal. Does this prove that this dinosaur gave birth to live young, instead of laying eggs? Or could it perhaps have swallowed the young animal whole?

ORNITHOLESTES

This dinosaur was given its evocative name – literally meaning 'bird-stealer' – because its large, grasping hands were thought to have been ideally suitable for grabbing at birds passing low overhead. It is often pictured clasping an unfortunate *Archaeopteryx* in its hands!

Unfortunately, this name does not stand up to close analysis, for two reasons. First, it has not been found in any of the same regions as *Archaeopteryx*, and second, it was eventually realised that the fossil remains named *Ornitholestes* were in fact of the same species as that named *Coelurus* in the 1880s.

Its proper name is therefore strictly *Coelurus* – but *Ornitholestes* seems to have stuck.

ORNITHOSUCHUS

Ornithosuchus probably included the young of both plant and flesh eating dinosaurs in its prey. Its name means 'bird crocodile', and its fossil remains have been found in Scotland.

GIANTS' GALLERY

MEGALOSAURUS

Bulky body: swayed from side to side during running.

Enormous, crocodile-like head.

Huge jaws and strong teeth for tearing flesh.

Arms: much weaker and smaller than hind legs.

Large, strong hind legs: could inflict stunning blow on prey.

Three clawed toes: typical of the *carnosaurs*.

Muscular tail: held up off the ground when running.

Footprints show that the feet landed one behind the other in running, with a slight turn inwards of the clawed toes.

FACTS AND FIGURES

Size: 4m tall, 6m long
Weight: 2.5 tonnes
Gait: Agile and quite fast
Diet: Meat
Meaning of name: Large lizard

(Megalosaurus was the first dinosaur to be named, in 1824. This explains why it is called 'large lizard', when in fact it is smaller than some of the other dinosaurs.)

ALLOSAURUS

This picture of a family group of *Allosaurus* ripping and slashing into the huge prey they have just downed, really says it all about this awesome beast. The dominant predator of its period, it was massive and tremendously strong. And just look at those jaws . . .

After the predators had taken their fill, they would rest, and scavengers – for instance a flock of *pterosaurs* – would move in for their share of the kill.

GORGOSAURUS

At 12 metres long and 4.5 metres tall, *Gorgosaurus* was even bigger than its ancestor *Allosaurus,* and it had certainly inherited the family's vicious traits!

When you see books full of dinosaur pictures, it is all too easy to get the impression that they all lived at the same time, and in the same places. What a wild party that would have been! The truth is that dinosaurs existed over such an unimaginably long time – 140 million years – that literally hundreds of millions of years – and thousands of miles – often separated the different species which evolved. *Gorgosaurus,* for instance, existed some 40 or so million years after its ancestor *Allosaurus.*

SPINOSAURUS

Spinosaurus lived in Egypt, and it is an interesting branch of the *carnosaur* family tree.

Its front legs were much more sturdy than most of the other flesh eaters, and it probably rested on all fours quite often, though it would have adopted the more usual stance, on its hind legs, when running in pursuit of prey.

The sail is a striking example of adaptation to a particular environment.

Just how did that sail work? Well, as usual, opinions differ! It may have been used to shade the sides of the body from the fierce daytime sun, and also in some way to store heat, for use later, in the cool of the night.

CERATOSAURUS

Its name means 'horned lizard', and there are no prizes for guessing why. On the end of its snout was a large bony horn, making it instantly recognisable. It was 5 metres long, and was one of the fiercest of all the flesh eaters. And that's certainly saying something!

WAS T REX A HUNTER?

On the opposite page is *Tyrannosaurus Rex,* possibly the best known dinosaur. It looks like a fierce hunter . . . but was it? Some experts believe that the massive weight of the animal and its two-legged stance would make it just too clumsy and slow to actually pursue and capture prey. Instead, they believe, it may have lived solely off carrion — which is the name for the flesh of a dead animal.

GIANTS' GALLERY

TYRANNOSAURUS REX

Huge eyes: your head would fit in the socket.

Powerful shoulder muscles: needed to raise the animal after lying down.

Weak arms.

Tail: helped with balance.

Tyrannosaurus Rex walked upright on hind legs.

Massive hind feet: footprint measured 75 cm both across and in length.

Deadly weapons: lethal, sharp claws on three toes.

Jaws: the business end of T Rex!

50 long, sharp teeth: tore away hunks of flesh from prey. These were probably swallowed whole, without chewing.

FACTS AND FIGURES

Size: 6 m tall, 15 m long
Weight: 8 tonnes
Gait: Awkward and slow, with short strides
Diet: Meat
Meaning of name:
King of the Tyrant Lizards

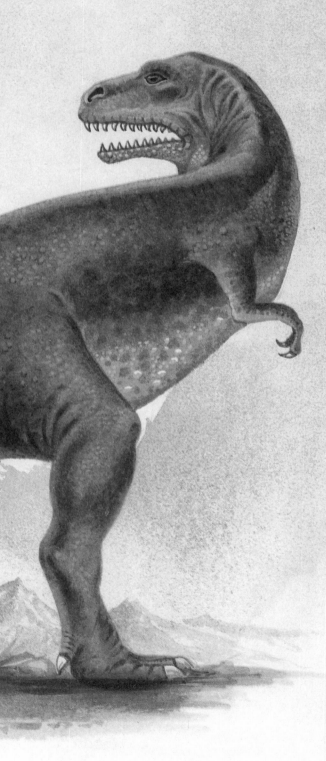

JUST IMAGINE . . .

When you read the vital statistics of some of the biggest dinosaurs, it's often difficult to visualise just how big these huge creatures really were. Sometimes it's helpful to imagine them alongside present day animals or objects.

STYRACOSAURUS was almost the size of an elephant.

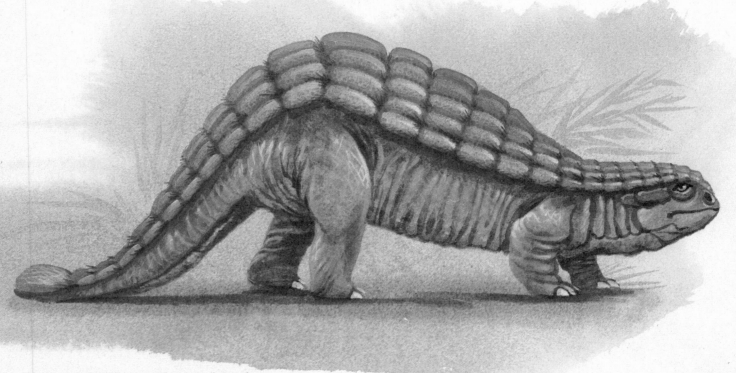

EUOPLOCEPHALUS was about the size of an estate car.

TRICERATOPS weighed about the same as an armoured tank.

TYRANNOSAURUS REX had teeth as long as a man's hand.

FOSSIL FACTS

Fossils provide an intricate record of the past, for those experts skilled enough to read it.

WHAT ARE FOSSILS?

Fossils are traces of living things from years long gone by.

It is not always the living material which becomes fossilised, but sometimes just an impression, for instance the vein outline of a leaf, or an animal's footprint.

Ammonites are common fossil finds, easily recognised by their distinctive shape.

By studying fossil footprints, measuring the distances between them, and making calculations based on the size of the animal, experts are sometimes even able to tell how fast an animal moved.

A VERY UNUSUAL FOSSIL!

In 1977 a dramatic fossil find was made in Siberia. A whole baby mammoth was discovered, embedded so deeply and firmly in ice that even its skin and soft tissues had been preserved for thousands of years.

The degree of preservation in some finds is astonishing. One example is the brilliantly-coloured yellow flies discovered in the Isle of Wight, and known to be 26 million years old. Their yellow pigment is chemically inert, and therefore has not changed since those flies were buzzing about their daily lives. In another well known example, fossil ink from *belemnites* was used to make drawings of their ink sacs.

WHAT CAN FOSSILS TELL US ABOUT DINOSAURS?

The answer to that one is: everything we know!

Fossil evidence, years of dedicated and painstaking research by experts all over the world, plus more than a little inspired guesswork, have combined to unite a patchwork of assorted facts into a clear chronological picture of the lifestyles of these intriguing animals.

Sometimes the fossil will be a single bone, or maybe a group of assorted bones which at first glance don't appear to bear any relation to each other. On other, much more rare occasions, a complete fossil skeleton may emerge from one site.

Whatever the find, it will have its own evidence to disclose, and it might even reveal facts for which a particular scientist has been searching for years.

Palaeontology has its roots firmly in the past, but it is painting a very dramatic picture for us to marvel over in the present. As for the future, well, one thing's sure: it has plenty of surprises in store, and a great deal more to reveal about the far-off age of the dinosaurs.

Sometimes a number of bones, perhaps found over a large area, can be reunited into a complete skeleton, such as this one of *Iguanodon*.

Iguanodon's thumb bone. At first only one was found, and people thought it must have belonged on the creature's snout.

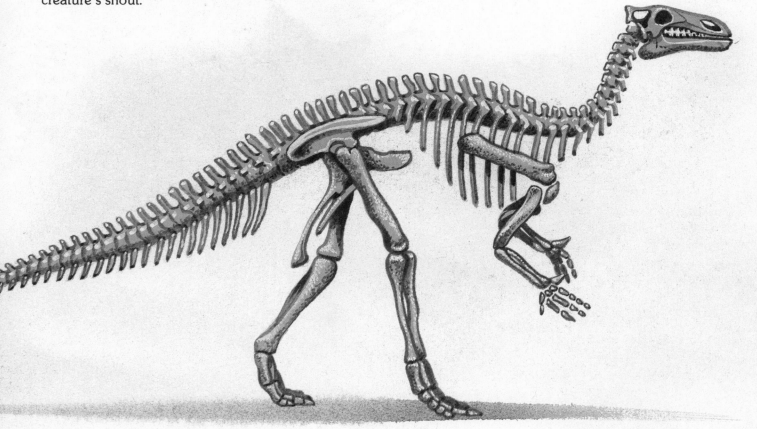

MORE UNANSWERED QUESTIONS

WHAT SOUNDS DID DINOSAURS MAKE?

This is a particularly intriguing question. Exciting cinema films such as *The Lost World* and *The Land That Time Forgot* would have us believe that the air fairly rang out with the bellows and cries of assorted dinosaurs, all apparently bent on breaking decibel records!

It might well have been just like that. The world might have been a very noisy place indeed.

It seems reasonable to assume that there would be a variety of sounds among the dinosaurs, just as there is among the animals of today, and that some would have made more noise than others.

Even today there are many gaps in our understanding of how animals communicate through sounds, but it may be that dinosaurs used different sounds for different purposes: as warnings to others, during mating, and so on.

HOW FAST DID DINOSAURS TRAVEL?

For once, we do have some answers to this one!

By studying fossil footprints, experts have been able to work out the probable speeds of a number of dinosaurs.

A huge flesh eater such as *Allosaurus* probably walked at around 5 m.p.h., which would be about double the speed of the massive plant eaters.

HOW FAST DID THEY GROW?

and

HOW LONG DID THEY LIVE?

Two more mysteries! We just don't know the answers to these two, though once again it seems logical to assume that there would be variations from animal to animal. Also, if you were a defenceless plant eater, how long you lived would depend to a great extent on how much of your bulky body you could hide behind a convenient tree, when a flesh eater came along!

DID MAN EVER SEE A DINOSAUR?

This has been the subject of much heated debate in recent years, because of the discovery of some interesting sets of footprints.

In each case – and there are several different sets – there appears to be a man's footprint walking beside a dinosaur track. Some people point to this as evidence that Man existed long before scientific reference books would have us believe.

The palaeontologists, however, think that the smaller prints were probably made by the forelimbs of a bipedal dinosaur, just touching the ground slightly as it walked along, bending forward to spread out its weight.

IN THE SKIES

Millions of years before the age of the dinosaurs, the first airborne creatures were insects, which unfortunately left little in the way of fossil remains. Next to take to the air were probably flying lizards, and of these we know a little more . . .

FLYING LIZARDS

Kuehnosaurus, shown here, was a fairly typical example of the flying lizards. It was not capable of true flapping flight, but had developed a useful gliding technique by using its wings rather like a parachute, to enable it to make slow, swooping descents from trees, during the course of which it could catch a good meal of insects.

There are lizards today which glide and swoop in much the same way.

PODOPTERYX

The name *Podopteryx* means 'foot wing', and as you can see it is apt, because its gliding membrane was attached to its fore and hind limbs. A wing like this would obviously be much more manoeuvrable, and the quite recent discovery of *Podopteryx* provided the probable 'missing link' between the flying lizards and the *pterosaurs* which would eventually dominate the skies.

Fossil remains of a reptile named *Longisquama* revealed elongated scales running the entire length of the animal's body. These spread out sideways and no doubt gave a parachute effect to enable the animal to glide. What was particularly interesting about these scales was that they might well have been the early forerunners of feathers.

THE PTEROSAURS

These strange, bat-like creatures were the terror of the skies for many millions of years.

They were mostly true, flapping fliers, and were no doubt extremely agile in the air. Their size varied a great deal, from small, almost sparrow-sized creatures, to fearsome-looking giants with a wingspan of 8 metres or more.

Many of the pterosaurs had sharp teeth, and they would probably have taken a variety of prey including insects, small mammals and reptiles, and fish.

PTERODACTYLUS

DIMOROHODON

Pterosaurs used their sharp claws to cling to trees.

PTERANODON

Many of the *pterosaurs* probably made clifftop roosts.

The finding of a species of *pterosaur* named *Sordes Pilosus* in 1971 gave dramatic new evidence about these creatures. This one was covered in thick hair, and it is likely that they all had a downy covering of some kind.

Many creatures had become airborne, but the important evolutionary distinction of being the world's first bird was left to . . .

ARCHAEOPTERYX

Archaeopteryx was first discovered in 1861 in Bavaria, and even in those days, when little was known of the early creatures, the find was recognised as a breakthrough.

For *Archaeopteryx* had feathers.

The first of the species may not have been very strong fliers, for their bones were solid and heavy – without the important air cavities which help birds of today to fly. They also had teeth, and front limbs, which have disappeared in the birds we know, but all the same they *were* birds!

It is possible that the male *Archaeopteryx* was more brightly coloured than the female, as with many birds of today.

Archaeopteryx means 'ancient feather'.

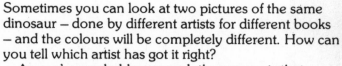

WHAT COLOUR WERE DINOSAURS?

Sometimes you can look at two pictures of the same dinosaur – done by different artists for different books – and the colours will be completely different. How can you tell which artist has got it right?

As you've probably guessed, the answer is that you *can't* tell, because no one knows exactly what colour the various different dinosaurs were: and quite probably, no one ever will.

One or two extremely rare exceptions go to prove the rule that fossil evidence does not reveal the colours of an animal in life.

Nevertheless, understanding dinosaurs is very often a matter of looking at the known facts and making an educated guess as to the unknown ones. And so it is with colour.

EDUCATED GUESSES

Colour is used in the animal world for a variety of reasons. In some birds, for instance, the male's bright plumage might be necessary to attract a mate – which might have been the case with *Archaeopteryx,* on the opposite page.

Another very important reason for colour differences is camouflage. An animal moving through the shadows of undergrowth stalking prey will be much more successful if its dappled coat blends in with its surroundings.

Try some educated guesses yourself. Think about a dinosaur, consider its way of life, and try to decide what colour you think it would have been. Then turn over, and see if you agree with our artist's ideas . . . !

Struthiomimus was an 'ostrich dinosaur', so called because its shape resembled that of an ostrich. Was its colouring like that of an ostrich too?

Was *Plateosaurus* discreetly shaded in greys and greens?

Did *Velociraptor* have tiger stripes?

Did *Allosaurus* sport leopard spots?

Was *Corythosaurus* zebra-striped in bronzes and tans?

Looking for a new spare time interest?
Why not try . . .

DINOSAURS AS A HOBBY

KEEP A DINOSAUR SCRAPBOOK

A scrapbook full of all sorts of dinosaur facts and figures can soon build up into a really interesting reference book. And it would be a great idea for a school project.

Spend some time planning your scrapbook out before you start pasting things in. Are you going to devote the whole scrapbook to your favourite dinosaur, for instance, or perhaps to a particular group? Or maybe you'd rather compile a more general scrapbook, perhaps subdivided into sections.

When you've decided that, you can start collecting things to paste in. Cuttings from newspapers are one idea (remember to make a note of the date), or you might have some comics with colour pictures of dinosaurs. Those would make a good start, and you could add interesting facts copied from reference books, in neat handwriting.

Have you visited a museum or any kind of exhibition connected with dinosaurs? Paste in your ticket, make a note of the date you went, and add your comments.

Lay your bits and pieces out on sheets of paper first, and move them round till you're pleased with the effect. Take a bit of time and trouble with your scrapbook – and the end product will be a really super book.

WHERE TO SEE DINOSAURS

Unfortunately, there just isn't anywhere you can see a real dinosaur. (Not that we know of, anyway!) But there are lots of interesting museums and other exhibitions, where you can see displays of various kinds.

There might well be a museum in your nearest large town which has a collection of fossils, for instance, and that would be a good place to start. If you are in London, the Natural History Museum has some excellent displays; and also interesting – though not exactly accurate! – are the large scale models of dinosaurs in Crystal Palace Park, made over a hundred years ago.

Going to the South Coast on holiday? Lyme Regis is famous for fossil finds. Visit the museum there, and The Fossil Shop – both fascinating to browse round.

AFTER THE DINOSAURS

When the dinosaurs became extinct, some 64 million years ago, it was the turn of other creatures to take advantage of the new feeding grounds, and to grow both in numbers and in different species.

Notably, the mammals flourished everywhere – and they came in all shapes and sizes.

SMILODON or SABRE-TOOTHED TIGER

With two elongated upper teeth growing to a length of 20 cm or more, *Smilodon* had its own built-in deadly weapons. Once it had made its kill though, its 'sabre teeth' would make chewing difficult, and it may have torn off chunks of flesh and swallowed them whole.

Surprisingly, *Smilodon* is not related to the big cats of today.

WILD DOGS

TOXODON

Packs of ferocious wild dogs roamed the lands – just as they still do in some parts of the world today – and mounted combined attacks on their victims, enabling them to prey on animals larger than themselves. An animal such as the peaceful, plant-eating *Toxodon,* shown here, would probably have had little chance of escape.

MEGATHERIUM

Aptly, the name of this huge, hairy mountain of a mammal means 'giant animal'. Standing 5 metres high on its hind legs to reach the branches of trees, it must have been a formidable sight, and though a peaceful creature would certainly have defended itself against attack with its massive sharp claws. It walked on all fours, and probably moved quite slowly – though not as slowly as its distant relative, the present day sloth.

UINTATHERIUM

Bigger than a rhinoceros, this unattractive-looking animal had no less than three pairs of bony 'horns', as well as two small, but very sharp, tusks. Although it would defend itself against an enemy – by charging, head down – it was really a peaceful plant eater, and despite its size its brain was very small.

PALAEOMASTODON

Related to a much bigger animal called *Mastodon, Palaeomastodon* looked rather like a baby elephant, at less than 2 metres high when fully grown. It lived in the region we now know as Egypt, feeding on the lush vegetation around lakes and rivers.

At over 5 metres tall, *Baluchitherium* was the largest known land mammal ever.

You need only think about the astonishing variety of mammals alive today to realise how successful this group of animals became. They developed into all manner of forms, with all manner of different ways of life. Some live in trees, some underground. Some eat meat, some eat plants, some eat insects. In some a physical ability is paramount – for instance speed or sight. In others the mental faculties are highly developed. This group of animals would ultimately lead to Man, who used his mental faculties most . . . and at times, least.

DIATRYMA

Diatryma was one of many fierce, carnivorous, flightless birds.

EOHIPPUS

Only about the size of a fox, *Eohippus* was the first horse. This tiny animal still had toes, but later they would develop into hooves.

GLYPTODON

A man could fit easily inside the shell of the huge, lumbering *Glyptodon*, and Early Man might well have done just that, if he came across an empty shell whose occupant had long since died. It would have been shelter, perhaps during a storm. A distant relative of today's armadillo, *Glyptodon* retreated into its impenetrable shell when under attack – and lashed out at enemies with its tail.

WOOLLY MAMMOTH

This great beast lived in the Steppes of Siberia, where its thick, shaggy coat gave protection against extreme cold. For part of the year the vegetation would be completely covered by snow, and the *Woolly Mammoth* used its immense, curved tusks to dig for food.

Early Man lived alongside some of these animals, and would have hunted some of them for food. He probably also made use of them in other ways, for instance using their skins for warmth.

GLOSSARY

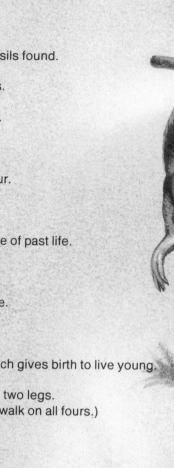

ammonite	Early shellfish – many fossils found.
amphibian	Animal which can live on land or in water.
anklyosaur	Armoured dinosaur.
belemnite	Early shellfish – many fossils found.
bipedal	Standing on two hind legs.
carnosaur	Big, flesh eating dinosaur.
cephalopod	Shellfish with tentacles.
ceratopsian	Horned and frilled dinosaur.
crossopterygian	Primitive fish.
fossil	Preserved remains or trace of past life.
hadrosaur	'Duck-billed' dinosaur.
invertebrate	Animal without a backbone.
ichthyosaur	Sea reptile.
mammal	Warm-blooded animal which gives birth to live young.
ornithopod	Dinosaur which walked on two legs. (Some *ornithopods* could walk on all fours.)

All dinosaurs belong to one of two main groups. The *ornithischians* is the name for the 'bird-hipped' dinosaurs, and others are *saurischians,* or 'lizard-hipped'.

palaeontology	Science of fossils.
paramammal	Animal with some features of mammals, some of reptiles.
placoderm	Early fish.
plesiosaur	Long-necked sea reptile.
pliosaur	Sea reptile.
pterosaur	Flying reptile.
protozoan	Micro-organism.
reptile	Cold-blooded, egg-laying animal.
sauropod	Four-footed dinosaur with long neck and small head.
scavenger	Animal which feeds on kills made by other animals.
stegosaur	Armoured dinosaur.
trilobite	Marine creature with hard 'shield' – many fossils found.
vertebrate	Animal with a backbone.

THE BIGGEST MYSTERY OF ALL . . .

Why did the dinosaurs die out?

Possibly the most intriguing of all the mysteries surrounding dinosaurs, this question has never been answered to the satisfaction of all the experts, even though numerous ingenious explanations have been put forward.

What we know for sure is that round about 64 million years ago the dinosaurs, a widespread and flourishing group of animals, quite simply disappeared from the earth, becoming extinct over a relatively short period of time. Birds, mammals, even other reptiles, survived. Why not the dinosaurs?

Great climatic changes have occurred throughout the history of our world. Did it quite simply become either too hot or too cold for the dinosaurs? Or was it that the climatic changes affected the plant life, making it unpalatable for the plant eaters? This would obviously have had a disastrous effect on the flesh eaters too, if their prey was substantially reduced in numbers. Or was it that great changes in the relative areas of land and water were happening just too quickly for the dinosaurs to adapt?

Various theories suggest an extra-terrestrial cause for the dinosaurs' extinction. Not the arrival of little green men (though that's an idea too!), but possibly a meteor crashing to earth, and throwing up debris on impact. This might have remained in the upper atmosphere, and blocked out the sunlight, thus greatly reducing plant life. Or could a comet have passed close to the earth, raising the temperature higher than the dinosaurs could tolerate?

Back on a down-to-earth level, it is possible that a deadly dinosaur disease swept the earth, wiping out the animals in such large numbers that breeding became impossible. Fossil evidence, informative as it is, might not reveal any traces of such a disease.

Maybe one day we will have conclusive proof to support one of these ideas, or indeed perhaps a completely new one will be put forward, on which all the experts can agree.

But for now the mystery remains . . .

Might even one real live dinosaur have survived?

Sad to say, the experts don't think so! They argue that if there was one around, surely by now we'd have some real evidence, and some verified sightings.

But of course there are still some remote, almost unexplored areas of the world, where it is *just possible* that a dinosaur or two could have survived . . .

And then of course there's *Nessiteras rhombopteryx.* That's the 'scientific' name of the Loch Ness Monster! Could this mysterious creature be a *plesiosaur,* left over from the age of the dinosaurs?

After all, from time to time other creatures believed extinct for millions of years — for instance the *coelacanth* — have been found alive and well, still going about their daily lives!

OAT

I wwent to the sppo.